ON THE
NATURE OF THOUGHT,
OR THE
ACT OF THINKING,
AND ITS
CONNEXION WITH A PERSPICUOUS SENTENCE.

By

JOHN HASLAM

Polonius—What do you read, my Lord?

Hamlet—Words, words, words.—*Act 2d.*

Mephistopheles.

"Im Ganzen—haltet euch an Worte!
Dann geht ihr durch die sichere Pforte
Zum Tempel der Gewissheit ein."

Schuler.

"Doch ein Begriff muss bey dem Worte seyn."

Mephistopheles.

"Schon gut! nur muss man sich nicht allzu ängstlich quälen,
Denn eben wo Begriffe fehlen,
Da stellt ein Wort zur rechten zeit sich ein.
Mit Worten lässt sich trefflich streiten,
Mit Worten ein System bereiten.
An Werte lässt sich trefflich glauben,
Von einem Wort lässt sich kein Iota rauben."—*Goëthe's Faust.*

"And when I have enumerated these, I imagine I have comprehended almost every thing which can enter into the composition of the intellectual life of man. With the single exception of reason, (and reason can scarcely operate without the intervention of language,) is there any thing more important to man, more peculiar to him, or more inseparable from his nature than speech? Nature indeed could not have bestowed on us a gift more precious than the human voice, which, possessing sounds for the expression of every feeling, and being capable of distinctions as minute, and combinations as intricate as the most complex instrument of music; is thus enabled to furnish materials so admirable for the formation of artificial language. The greatest and most important discovery of human ingenuity is writing; there is no impiety in saying, that it was scarcely in the power of the Deity to confer on man a more glorious present than Language, by the medium of which, he himself has been revealed to us, and which affords at once the strongest bond of union, and the best instrument of communication. So inseparable indeed are mind and language, so *identically one* are thought and speech, that although we must always hold reason to be the great characteristic and peculiar attribute of man, yet language also, when we regard its original object and intrinsic dignity, is well intitled to be considered as a component part of the intellectual structure of our being. And although, in strict application, and rigid expression, thought and speech always are, and always must be, regarded as two things metaphysically distinct,—yet there only can we find these two elements in disunion, where one or both have been employed imperfectly or amiss. Nay, such is the effect of the original unity or *identity* that, in their most extensive varieties of application, they can never be totally disunited, but must always remain inseparable, and every where be exerted in combination."—*Frederick Schlegel's Lectures on the History of Literature, (English Translation, 1818,) page 11.*

TO

MRS. HUNTER, DUNDEE.

My dearest Daughter,

This Essay on Thought *is appropriately dedicated to a lady of whom I am constantly thinking:—whose dutiful conduct, and filial affection, have rendered a protracted life the subject of consolation, under all its contingent miseries.*

*33, Great Ormond Street,
    June 1835.*

ON

THE NATURE OF THOUGHT,

&c. &c. &c.

In our survey of the Creation endowed with life and intellect, we are impelled to the conclusion, that the human mind is, beyond all comparison, the most perfect specimen that the Divine Author has chosen to allot to his creatures. The history of our species unfolds the splendid catalogue of man's achievements: many monuments, reared by his patriotism and piety, and elaborated by his tasteful ingenuity, that have resisted the corrosions of time, and the spoliations of conquest, remain in our possession: and we still preserve those intellectual treasures that embalm the poetry, the eloquence, and the wisdom of the enlightened nations of antiquity. These are, deservedly, the models we have endeavoured to imitate, and they have even been considered the boundaries of attainment: but a new epoch has arisen, distinguished for the cultivation of that which tends to ultimate advantage, where the mind, confiding in its native energies, and exercising its own thought on human affairs, has been less disposed to submit to the dictates of authority.

At this period we possess abundant facilities for the acquirement of valuable knowledge: under this system, the mental faculties have been directed to their proper objects, and the time consumed in teaching has been considerably abbreviated. This abridgement of the usual course of education has conduced to the neglect of that classical learning, which required a painful and enduring attention, even for many years, to two languages that have ceased to be spoken, and are only addressed to the eye in written character. It is in no manner intended to under-rate the value of classical literature, the constituent of a scholar, and the passport and ornament of a gentleman; but to introduce a very probable opinion, that few of those who have devoted many of the most productive years of their existence to the Greek and Latin writers, ever attain a critical knowledge of those tongues: and that the substance of morals, wisdom, and even the elegant turns of expression, may be more certainly conveyed through the medium of the best translations, which we now possess, and the performance of which has occupied a large portion of the time of accomplished scholars. This conversion of talent to that which is useful, and productive of emolument, has given a more energetic impulse to the mind, and accelerated that march of which we now so justly boast: but it cannot be denied, that in the rapidity of our advancement, and flushed with the ardent hope of arriving at our destination, we have bestowed but little notice on the machinery that urged us forwards, or contemplated the scenery through which we passed.

Most persons concur that the human mind is the noblest subject of investigation; but few will be at the trouble of undertaking its analysis. With the multitude there is neither leisure nor inclination, and the doctrines that have been dictated concerning our intellectual faculties and their operations, have tended rather to stifle than to promote inquiry. It is therefore unnecessary to enumerate the catalogue of illustrious names whose contradictory systems have created suspicion and distaste in the student. The science that has been improperly termed Metaphysics, ought to be considered a branch of human physiology, not abstracted from, but in this state of existence, connected with the phenomena of life. The citations on the reverse of the Title-page, to which many more might have been added, clearly shew that the doctrine of words being the elements of Thought, did not originate from my own conjecture or inference, and, consequently, that the endeavour to investigate its truth has been the sole object of my research; under the persuasion that, if ideas were inadequate, words only remained to afford the solution of this important process. The necessary connexion of thought with the construction of a perspicuous sentence, has not, to my knowledge, been previously noticed.

We are said to THINK on certain subjects, and this process is confessed to require an intense exertion of our intellectual faculties: but for this operation, the materials have not been clearly specified, nor the manner of the elaboration defined. It has been held, that our thoughts are produced by some mysterious assemblage and arrangement of IDEAS, which the mind or soul performs by a dexterous and imperceptible contrivance; although we are conscious of all our acts of intelligence, and on a moment's consideration it will be evident, that such intelligence would be useless without our consciousness.

Mr. Locke, whose name can never be mentioned without a grateful recollection for the instruction he has afforded us, and for the candour with which he has recorded the difficulties that obstructed the progress of his inquiries, has employed this ideal system most extensively: but it is evident, that he felt the obscurity of his own definition. In his Introduction to the Essay, p. 5, 6th edition, he says, "Before I proceed on what I have thought on this subject, I must here in the entrance beg pardon of my reader, for the frequent use of the word Idea, which he will find in the following Treatise. It being that term which, I think, serves best to stand for whatsoever is the object of the understanding, when a man thinks. I have used it to express whatever is meant by Phantasm, Notion, Species, OR WHATEVER IT IS, which the mind can be employed about in thinking; and I could not avoid frequently using it." Dr. Reid follows nearly in the same track:—"It is a fundamental principle of the Ideal system, that every object of thought, must be an *impression* or an *Idea*, that is, a *faint copy* of some preceding impression."—*Inquiry into the Human Mind on the Principles of Common Sense*, 1765, p. 41.

The doctrine of Innate Ideas having been deservedly exploded, it follows that these Ideas must be derived from our intercourse with the world we inhabit. For this purpose we are furnished with five senses, from each of which we obtain a separate and different kind of intelligence, which is denominated Perception. The perceptions of the Eye, under an attentive inspection, leave on the Sensorium a phantasm or Idea of the object, a vivid memorial of that which has been perceived; but the other senses do not convey any similar phantasm.[1] The doctrine of Ideas appears to have been countenanced, and reconciled under all its difficulties, from a presumed spiritual operation and guidance in the act of thinking, and especially to an implacable aversion to any explanation that might be deemed to savour of *materialism*. This term, the denunciation of the pious, the convenient obloquy of the ignorant, being equal in its sweeping persecution, to the horrible word craven, demands a brief and modest exposition. That we exist in a material world, will scarcely be denied, and it is a fair inference, that the annihilation of matter would involve our globe and its inhabitants in equal destruction. Of this matter, the concentrated power of man cannot create nor exterminate a single atom. The human body is a material fabric: the brain and nerves, together with those delicate organs that are the instruments of our perceptions,—whereby we receive light, detect fragrance, apprehend sounds, relish viands, and enjoy the gratifications of contact, are all of material structure: and when that state, called Death, has ensued, their offices cease, and they undergo the decompositions to which all animal matter is subjected.

The *Capacities*, by which we feel, experience pleasure and pain, perceive, remember, exercise volition, and become conscious, may be termed Spiritual, or if it be preferred, Divine endowments; and it is not probable that we shall ever detect the immediate agency by which these operations are performed. The state of *Life*, the indispensable medium for the display of the phenomena of intelligence in our present condition of existence, is equally inscrutable by human sagacity, although different hypotheses have been adventured for its solution.

To account for the harmonious concurrence of motions and processes that distinguish living animals, a MATTER OF LIFE has been supposed, and its nature conjectured to be some modification[2] of electricity or galvanism, and which being unsupported, is not deserving of further comment. Another sect of physiologists has conceived that life is the immediate result of a particular organization; but they are unable to demonstrate that any arrangement of parts is consequently endowed with vital actions. This arrangement of particular tissues, may be absolutely necessary for the performance of various functions in the living state: but this is altogether different from the energy or cause that excites the action. A violin and its bow are prepared to "discourse most excellent music," yet they are mute until guided by the skilful hands of the performer. When death ensues from many diseases, the organization remains, for without this concession our anatomical knowledge must be very imperfect. Thus the nature of life, whether it be developed in the vegetable creation, or display its admirable complications in the higher animals, is inexplicable on any of the principles that regulate our philosophy, and can only be referred to the contrivance and disposition of infinite wisdom: yet the vehicle in which these stupendous operations are conducted owns a material basis: even the confused mass that composes the earth we tread on possesses certain intrinsic properties. Every atom is subjected to definite regulation, and without exaggeration, may be considered endowed with instinctive tendency to coalesce or disunite under favourable opportunities, and the correct observation of these habitudes, constitutes the foundations of chemical science. When the power and intelligence of the supreme Artificer is conspicuous in the ultimate particles of matter, we ought to be more temperate in our invectives against the doctrine of materialism.

Ideas have been generally employed, and held competent, by many of the tribe of metaphysicians, to explain the phenomena and operations of our intellectual nature: but they have failed in the attempt. They have endeavoured to confer on them an agency they do not possess, and have given the mind a dominion over them that it cannot exert.[3] Ideas are the memorial phantasms of visual perception, a largess bestowed, perhaps exclusively, on the sense of sight, and this bounty contributes essentially to the acquirement and retention of knowledge. They are the unfading transcripts of vision, and they exhibit the original picture to the retrospect of memory. They are but little under the immediate direction of the will, and cannot be arbitrarily summoned or dismissed, but owe their introduction to a different source, to be explained hereafter. They perform important offices, although they are not the materials to rear and consolidate the edifice of thought.

Those writers on the human mind who have adhered to the doctrine of Ideas, and have been the advocates for the Spirituality of Thought, have insufficiently considered, or held in subordinate regard, Language; the prominent criterion, by which a human being is proudly elevated above the rest of the animated creation. Speech, and its representation by characters, are exclusively comprehensible by man; and these have been the sources of his vast attainments and rapid progression. The ear receives the various intonations that convey intelligence, and the characters or symbols of these significant sounds are detected by the human eye. Some of the more docile animals have been supposed capable of comprehending the meaning of a few individual words, but no one worthy of belief, has affirmed that they could understand a sentence or distinct proposition: still less, has any person, however confiding in the marvellous, ever ventured to assert that they were able to read. The important feature, and obvious utility of language, consists in the commutation of our perceptions for a significant sound or word, which by convention may be communicated to others, bearing a common and identical meaning. In this manner we become intelligible to each other, by the transmission and reception of these articulate and significant sounds. Words are not only the representatives of the perceptions we receive through the medium of our five senses, but likewise of many internal feelings, passions, and emotions, together with all that the *Mind* (the aggregate of capacity and acquired intelligence) has elaborated. The result of this commutation renders the word the intelligible substitute for the thing perceived, so that the presence of the object recalls its name, and the name when uttered excites the immediate recollection of the absent object. This reciprocal substitution or mutual exchange, forms the basis, and affords a reason for Language. Whoever will take the trouble to watch the progress of the child from the commencement of its efforts to speak, will be surprised with its display of curiosity and intelligence. It feels delighted with the existence it enjoys, and with the power its senses possess to examine the objects of the world that surrounds it. Every organ, in succession, is occupied in noticing the wonders and mysteries that are presented. This incessant, but silent play of perception, proceeds until a sound, often repeated, interests the sense of hearing, and although at first dimly comprehended, is meant to represent some present object or person, and which, by an excitement little understood, urges the effort of imitation. The success of intelligible pronunciation impels it forward to other attempts, *vires acquirit eundo*, and in a time comparatively short, it accumulates a copious vocabulary. These are the incipient efforts to establish that commutation of the object of perception for the word, on which the structure of language is erected. It is unnecessary further to trace these dawnings of speech, or to describe the satisfaction that is felt, when the child by this commutation of perceptions for words, can communicate the wonders it has seen, the delicacies it has tasted, or the flattering commendations bestowed on its person and accomplishments. This commutation confers additional satisfaction by being enabled to invest the object of immediate perception with an appropriate and intelligible name. Thus by the repeated exercise of this commutation, which soon becomes confirmed into habit, we speak of the past, by the assistance of memory, with the correctness and feeling of the present. At a certain age we learn to discriminate the characters that compose words, (letters)—the order in which they are placed, (orthography,) and with greater difficulty, the position of these words, to convey a definite and connected meaning. When reading has been fully attained, it must be recollected that all the sentences in the volume we peruse, are composed of individual words, that are examples of the commutation mentioned; and although the objects are absent, and the actions have been long since performed, often for centuries, we are interested in the narrative, and bestow the appropriate tribute of sympathy or admiration. Words, thus impregnated with definite meaning, become the floating currency of the mind, are the efficient materials of Thought, and of its perspicuous expression.

It has been frequently remarked, that the mind is more delighted by making distant excursions, than in the examination of surrounding objects, or of those directly obvious. Such immediate assistance for the pursuit and development of this inquiry is presented in two remarkable instances, where Nature digresses from her usual course, and which are not of rare occurrence. 1st. Some persons are born with their ears impervious to sound, and as language is acquired by imitation,[4] such as are deaf, remain mute or dumb.[5] With the exception of the sense of hearing, they are like animals the creatures of perception. Some have displayed considerable curiosity in examining objects by the eye, and by the organs of touch, taste, and smell: but they do not, with these elements of knowledge, progressively advance in intelligence, until they have been circuitously taught the characters that are the constituents of words, and also to comprehend, that the word itself is the commuted substitute for the object perceived. Notwithstanding these deficiencies, and disqualifications for human intercourse, these deaf, and consequently dumb persons, must be, in a very high degree, the subjects of Ideas, or of those phantasms that are associated with visual perception.

The second instance, is of those who are born blind, and continue sightless through life. A person under such total privation of vision, must be exempt from those phantasms or Ideas, that are connected with, or are the residuary contingents on visual perception: yet the blind acquire speech, when young, with equal facility, as the children who enjoy sight; but visible objects must, to them, be abstract or complex terms, as all such necessarily are, that cannot be the objects of perception. The other sensitive organs, and especially the touch, to a limited extent, become the substitutes for visual defect, although they are no actual compensations for sight. By models the blind can become acquainted with alphabetic characters, and unite them into words: and in the same manner discriminate, and record the musical notes. Some of the blind have become highly intelligent, and have excelled in conversational acuteness; and as human beings have left the deaf and dumb in the rear, notwithstanding the latter are furnished with all the *Ideas* that can be inherited from sight. This constant employment of words, impregnated with meaning, affords the blind considerable facility in acquiring information by pertinent questions, and enables him to communicate his thoughts with precision and correctness. These words, and the intelligence that resides in them, are the only sources of his knowledge, (his perceptions being commuted for words,) and the meaning they import is all that it is necessary for him to comprehend. It may here be repeated that the capacity by which man exclusively exercises the range of thought by sounds that are significant, and receives from others the same oral intelligence, has no material basis that we can possibly detect or logically infer: but must be considered an endowment of infinite power and wisdom.

Before we attribute such vast powers to these Ideas or phantasms, the shadows of visual perception, it will be convenient to inquire into their nature, and endeavour to ascertain the laws by which they are regulated. In that state of mental relaxation, when the intellect is not intently occupied on any particular subject, numberless phantasms will involuntarily intrude: for, during the time we are awake, the mind is never wholly unoccupied, and such irregular presentations of Ideas constitute our reveries. However these ignes fatui may glimmer in their wanderings, tumultuously assemble, or abruptly depart; such confluence or dispersion contributes nothing to effective thought. As far as these Ideas or phantasms, the obsequious shadows of visual perception, can be traced, they are incapable of being summoned to appear by any voluntary command; but are consequently revived by the term or word for which the perception is commuted. Thus, having previously noticed them with attention, when we speak of St. Paul's Cathedral or Westminster Abbey, the attendant visions of these buildings immediately arise, and we are impressed with a memorial picture in conjunction with, and through the intervention of the word. The will possesses no power to unite or separate Ideas; they adhere to, and remain the unalterable deposits of perception. Let it next be asked, what human purpose can be effected by their sole agency? On those solemn occasions when we address our prayers to the Divine Source, can these effusions of grateful feeling, and humble petition, be conveyed in phantasms? Does not the lamenting and repentant sinner emphatically articulate his anxious supplications? Can any human contract be concluded by mere Ideas, or any system of jurisprudence be established on such visionary basis? Ideas therefore cannot enable us to perform our duty towards God, or our neighbour.[6]

In pursuing this important subject, the candid confession of Mr. Locke bewrays his distrust of the powers and efficiency of his favourite Ideas. "To form a clear notion of *Truth*, it is very necessary to consider Truth of Thought, and Truth of words distinctly one from another: but yet it is very difficult to treat of them asunder. Because it is unavoidable, in treating of mental propositions to make use of words; and then the instances given of *mental* propositions, cease immediately to be barely mental, and become *verbal*. For a mental proposition, being nothing *but a bare consideration of the Ideas*, as they are in our minds *stripped* of names, they lose the nature of purely mental propositions, as soon as they are put into words. And that which makes it *yet harder* to treat of mental and verbal Propositions separately, is, that most men, if not all, in their THINKING, and reasonings within themselves, make use of Words, instead of Ideas, at least when the subject of their meditation contains in it complex Ideas. Which is a great evidence of the imperfection and uncertainty of our Ideas of that kind, and may, if attentively made use of, serve for a mark to shew us, what are those things, we have clear and perfect established Ideas of, and what not."—*Vol.* II. *C.* 5, *p.* 195. Mr.

Locke was a patient and acute observer of that which passed in his own mind, when he strictly meditated any particular subject: and in this process he was likewise aware, in common with others, that he employed *words* instead of Ideas in his thinking and reasoning within himself. By Ideas alone, he confesses that he could not advance; and for this evident reason, because Ideas are incapable of being communicated to others, or received by ourselves, excepting through a verbal medium. There is no evidence of Thought without it be perspicuously expressed in words addressed to the ear, or by their characters presented to the eye; and the vain consciousness we may feel that our mind is teeming with important Thoughts, is little to be relied on, until we are capable of expressing them orally, or exhibiting them in writing. It has been a prevailing opinion with those attached to the Ideal doctrine, and who are advocates for the spiritual process of Thought, that the Idea is first conceived mentally, and subsequently, by some process not explained, invested with the corresponding expression. It is however certain that the word itself, with the meaning that is attached to it, must be previously acquired, and thoroughly comprehended, before the abstract Idea, or naked Thought, can select the befitting expression, and ransack the vast range of a copious vocabulary. The believers in the extreme rapidity of thought to which we shall presently advert, must be alarmed at this manner of explanation, which necessarily constitutes Thought a two-fold process, and consequently would consume, at least double the time for its disclosure. Perhaps in all instances the phraseology we employ, like our manners, is derived from the society we frequent: that which is imbibed from persons of good education bears the stamp of superior discrimination and correctness, contrasted with the rude dialect of the vulgar: but it still remains unsolved, by what means these phantasms, or Ideas, accommodate themselves with the appropriate words to express the Thoughts they have conceived.

Can it be supposed that the abstract, naked, and incommunicable conception possesses an innate sagacity to clothe itself with a verbal garb, at best of capricious and transient fashion?

"Multa renascentur, quæ jam cecidere,
cadentque

> Quæ nunc sunt in honore vocabula, si
> volet usus,
> Quem penes arbitrium est, et jus et
> norma loquendi."

It is certain that Ideas may exist in the mind, as the connected results, and enduring phantasms of visual perception, independently of words, and such condition is exemplified in those born deaf, who are consequently dumb: to whom the business of life is a mere pantomime, who only communicate the impulses of passion, and expose their want of comprehension.

> "In dumb significants proclaim their
> Thoughts."—*Henry VIth.*

From these examples it appears that a human being may possess a multitude of Ideas, and yet be wholly ignorant of language: and in the instances of those born blind, he may acquire speech to its fullest extent without having any Ideas, which therefore cannot be considered the necessary instruments of Thought. Thus, the presumed mutual intercourse, and reciprocal correspondence between Ideas and words is a very disputable conclusion.

When the Idea or phantasm that is connected with visual perception appears, in consequence of the word being mentioned (which by commutation is its substitute), the presentation is immediate. He who has visited and attentively noted interesting scenes, mountainous districts, cataracts or prospects, when they are mentioned, will have their phantasms or pictured images occur to him, and he will be aware of them, like the intrusion of a sudden flash. From this phenomenon the generally received opinion of the *rapidity* of *Thought* may in all probability have originated.

All popular and settled notions, however unfounded, like prejudices early imbibed, are with difficulty eradicated. Among these may be instanced the dictum of the astonishing rapidity of Thought, which is almost proverbial, and generally believed: even Mr. Tooke, Vol. I., p. 28, conforms to this established maxim. "Words have been called *winged*: and they well deserve that name, when their abbreviations are compared with the progress which speech could make without these inventions; but when compared with the *rapidity* of *thought*, they have not the smallest claim to that title." By calculation, the progress of light from the sun and other luminaries is said to be ascertained; and likewise the rate at which sound travels: but hitherto no contrivance has been fabricated to estimate the rapidity of thought. If the succession of our thoughts should be more rapid than they can be distinctly apprehended, confusion must ensue, and their rapidity would render them useless. Our perceptions are regulated by the same law. If the prismatic colours be painted on a surface which is revolved with great rapidity, the individual colours will not be apparent. The succession of sounds to a definite number, may be severally distinguished, in a certain interval: but if the succession be increased beyond the power of discrimination, they will impress the ear as one uniform sound. The same principle must regulate our thoughts, whether they be composed of Ideas or words, or, if it be possible, of both jumbled together. It does not appear that our thoughts for any useful purpose, which must imply their communication to others, or for a record in written characters, *can* be more rapid than the intelligible pronunciation of the words themselves, and which, when delivered in quick succession, leave the short-hand-writer behind.[7]

As Ideas can be nothing more than the mere phantasms attendant on visual perception, which, like the perceptions of the other senses, are commuted for words, that, by the aid of memory, recall in their absence the objects that have been perceived; it would be difficult to suppose that Ideas could fortuitously or voluntarily assemble in a more rapid succession, than the words for which they have been commuted, without producing confusion. It frequently happens to inexperienced persons, in giving evidence before a legal tribunal, or in addressing a popular assembly, that they cannot proceed; and they are generally disposed to interpret this failure, to their thoughts occurring in a succession too rapid for their utterance. Allowing the apology to be correct, it is a proof that such rapidity is inconvenient, and renders the Thought wholly useless if it cannot be communicated.

When we attentively measure the steps of our own minds in the act of thinking, and also observe the progress of others, it will be found that effective Thought does not result from this rapid and tumultuous rush of Ideas; but is a very deliberate, and in many cases painful elaboration: and must, when committed to writing, be subjected to subsequent revisals and repeated corrections, and which must be applied to the *words* constituting the sentence in which the thought is contained. From this general view of the subject, it is concluded that Ideas, the residuary phantasms of visual perception, cannot directly constitute or become the immediate instruments of Thought.

The present Essay being considered an humble attempt to investigate a portion of intellectual physiology, an apology will scarcely be deemed necessary for a short digression to inquire into the powers and faculties of the human mind: and which, when determined, may be viewed as the alphabet of mental science.

Systems prematurely constructed, and under the impression of authority, have been especial impediments to our intellectual progress: and this truth has been remarkably exemplified in the works that have treated of the human mind. In the numerous treatises on this subject that have issued from the press, there is but little agreement concerning these powers or faculties, and it is evident that a definite number must be required: some writers enumerate more, others less, and it is not unusual for some of these metaphysical projectors to split a single and presumed faculty into a variety of subdivisions. To the acute and patient observer, it will appear that the operations of Nature are contrived with admirable simplicity; but man, in his endeavours to explain them, has generally resorted to a mysterious and discouraging complexity. Thus, as might be expected, the same faculty, according to different authorities, has dissimilar energies,—one is detected to encroach on the boundary of another, and when the mechanism of mind, fabricated by these scholastic dictators, is attempted to be set in motion, it is found incapable of working. For the grand moving power we have an undefined, and consequently unintelligible doctrine of *Ideas*, of supposed spiritual and directing agency; the admission of which would destroy the responsibility of a human being both here and hereafter, and degrade his ennobled condition to the instinct of the speechless brute. To endow these insubstantial and reflected phantasms with some activity and mimic play, a theory of the *association of Ideas* has been erected, without having previously established that they are capable of such confederation. A wearisome catalogue of faculties, many of which are conjectural, has been enumerated; Abstraction, Conception, Contemplation, Consciousness, Comparison, Imagination, Judgment, Memory, Recollection, Reminiscence, Retention, Perception, Sensation, Reflection, Thought, Understanding, Volition, and many others that caprice has created, or a subtle discrimination helped to multiply. These are the materials out of which scholastic metaphysicians have fashioned their unresembling model, and deserted Nature. It is not intended in this abbreviated essay to settle the pretensions of these numerous faculties, the discussion of which would require an ample volume: and the award might probably be protracted, till the claim was forgotten. When we contemplate the dexterities that the hand performs, and the monuments of skill and taste that it has elaborated; it would only create unnecessary distinctions to affirm that it possessed the faculties of sculpturing, painting, writing, spinning, weaving, sewing, and numberless other manipulations: besides those that ulterior discoveries may enable it to accomplish. However profuse these constructors of the mind may have been in the accumulation of its component faculties, they appear to have little regarded language, its most prominent and important feature; *the universal menstruum of intelligence, and accredited currency for the circulation and exchange of thought*. There are two faculties or capacities that are peculiar to the human intellect, by which our species has attained a supremacy that leaves all other animated beings in a distant rear: the possession of which has rendered man a progressive being, and the race of animals so nearly stationary, that however they may be tortured into improvement, they feel no emulation to proceed, and the acquirement perishes where the brute expires. These undisputed faculties are Speech, with its recording characters, and the comprehension of numbers, the powerful sources of that pre-eminence which man has already attained, and to which he must be indebted for his further advancement.

As Ideas are wholly incompetent to explain the process of thought, the next inquiry will be, whether words are capable of affording the adequate solution. For this purpose, the simple experiment would be sufficient; and as we are conscious, under due attention of all the acts that the mind performs, every person, in proportion to his habits of deliberately noting that which passes within himself, will be enabled to institute this examination. It is however to be lamented, that Thought is not the constant or habitual exercise of the mind on the phenomena of Nature, the occurrences of life, or the subjects we listen to and peruse: but is only occasionally awakened by difficulties, excited by contention, or invoked by the promise of fame and by the hope of emolument. The usual course of education is but little calculated to promote the habitudes of thinking, and especially that teaching where authority dictates, and demonstration is neglected. Much of this instruction is enforced by degradation and terror; and the pupil, at an early age, is compelled to swallow doctrines which he is unable to comprehend, and consequently cannot digest, except through the peptic assistance of the scourge: and which, when matured by manhood, and enlightened by reason, he is forced to reject.

Thought requires knowledge as its basis, and in proportion to its extent on any given subject, the investigation will be productive. This knowledge may be acquired by conversation, reading, or experiment, and these require Language, or a composition of words. Knowledge supplies the materials for

thought, and every thought must be a distinct
proposition, or sentence composed of words.
A single word, although it possesses a distinct
meaning, cannot constitute a thought, which
implies a separate proposition or inference
contained in a sentence: still less can it be
supposed to result from an individual
phantasm or Idea. When it is considered that
language is composed of words adapted by
position to represent all the phenomena and
contingencies of human affairs, and that we
employ them, *by commutation*, for all that we
can experience as sentient and intellectual
beings, we shall be able to understand that
they are the mental currency previously
described, and that they are the only
instruments of intelligence to which we can
resort for the communication of our thoughts,
or for the process of their elaboration. They
must be expressed in words, and by words
prepared for such expression. Without
attempting to investigate the different kinds of
words, or parts of speech, the province of
general or philosophical grammarians, whose
unsettled disputes still perplex the patient and
modest inquirer, it will be sufficient to remark
that we possess words adapted to convey all
the shades of opinion and degrees of feeling:
and when these words, under the guidance of

acquired knowledge, are perspicuously arranged into a proposition or sentence, they constitute Thought: and the act of thinking consists in their correct selection and arrangement for the purpose of promulgation by speech or writing, and which is very properly termed composition. When we reflect, that from our infancy to the natural decline of our intellectual powers, we are employed, during our waking hours, in the exercise of language;[8]—by conversation, often desultory, where we range through a variety of topics, as the bird sports from branch to twig; to the more deliberate act of composition, where the mind enduringly broods on the subject;—or when we read, and attentively consider the thoughts of others:— these occupations contribute to augment our vocabulary, and fix the meaning of the words we employ. By these words, and the intelligence that resides in them, although many centuries have passed by, we participate, and feel impregnated with the pure and exalted spirit that conceived the Iliad and Odyssey. Time has not diminished the vigour or impaired the beauty of those memorials that have survived the extinction of the Grecian states, and the glory of the eternal city; and such is the luminous correspondence of Language, that by transfusion into our vernacular idiom, we may receive a satisfactory measure of the original inspiration. Let it be kept in view, that Ideas, the frail associates of a perception, possess no permanence, are incapable of being transferred, and must fade away when our existence terminates. It is the word that forms the nucleus, and contains the intellectual deposit, that may become the inheritance of future generations.

This process, in no manner or degree tends to subvert the spiritual nature of Thought, which has its source in the capacities whereby we perceive, remember, and comprehend that significant sounds or words are the commuted representatives of the objects of intelligence. The perceptive organs of many animals are more exquisitely endowed than man, and their local memory more retentive; yet they are wholly incapable of comprehending language or calculating numbers;—capacities by which the Creator has exclusively dignified the human race.

It may excite some surprise that an Essay on Thought should be connected with the construction of a perspicuous sentence. To explain this conjunction, it may be urged, that there can be no evidence of thought, until it is promulgated by speech or written character: and, on all important occasions, such communications of meaning become absolutely necessary. Acquiescence or dissent may indeed be tacitly conveyed, by holding up the hand, or by ballot, without condescending to offer any verbal reasons for the adoption or rejection of the proposed measure. Affirmation or negation does not in any manner constitute Thought; such determination may result from caprice, from ignorance, or from prejudice, without the slightest consideration. Thought requires some proposition clearly conceived and perspicuously expressed in a sentence; and the clearness of the Thought will be ascertained by the perspicuity of its verbal expression. There may be some difficulty respecting the precise meaning of individual words, arising from the corruptions of the ignorant; but more especially from the perversions of writers who have been deemed authorities. This distortion of the original sense, is, in a certain degree, incidental to all living languages, which being in childhood acquired by the ear, the learner is compelled to adopt the signification of words, and employ the current phraseology of those with whom he associates. When he is subsequently taught to speak and write by rule, or grammatically, generally at an age anterior to the exercise of reason, he is coerced to imbibe that which is forced in the way of instruction. Even at a more advanced period the student cannot readily comprehend how a perspicuous sentence is formed by the position of individual words, each bearing a distinct signification, which it is presumed must be the fact: but Mr. Dugald Stewart, in his *Philosophical Essays*, *p.* 155, has introduced a doctrine entirely opposite to this well-founded position. "So different is all this from the fact, that our words when examined *separately*, are *often* as completely insignificant as the letters of which they are composed: deriving their meaning *solely* from the connexion, or relation in which they stand to others."

For the memory of Mr. Stewart, in common with his surviving pupils, I feel the reverence that is due to a learned, eloquent and amiable instructor, although I may now differ with him in many essential points relating to his philosophy of the human mind. The fact, that every word possesses a distinct meaning, appears to constitute one of the foundations of language: and it is impossible to conceive that any word, in itself completely insignificant, can impart signification to others; that which it does not contain cannot be communicated. The reservation contained in the word *often*, implies that some words really are significant; but no directions are given how to discover, and select from the copious vocabulary of our language, such as are impregnated with meaning, in order to expunge those that are insignificant. When we consult Dr. Johnson's Dictionary, we find that the greater part of the words enumerated in his ample collection, instead of being senseless, enjoy an exuberance of meaning. Thus the verb to think has ten significations; the substantive Thought (the preterite of the verb), 12; Something, n. s., 5; Nothing, n. s., 11; Smooth, adj., 6; Rough, adj., 12; To stand, v. n., 69; To run, v. n., 62; Empty, adj., 9; Full, adj., 15; Beginning, n. s., 5; End, n. s., 20; Before, prepos., 12; After, prep., 6. However strange, or perhaps ludicrous, these numbers may seem, yet, in the progress of language from barbarism to refinement, from the assumed authority of writers, this accumulation of meanings is inevitable. However precise the primitive signification of words may have been, imagination, passion, or feeling would readily train them to deflect from their original import, under the effusions of the "poet, the lunatic, or the lover." A correct etymology would unfold the rude and simple origin of many words, that our Anglo-saxon, and Norman ancestors have bequeathed to us; although we are now but little sensible of the legacy; as the great mass feels no inclination to revert to the source of derivation. Many have been distorted by corruption, and these are the most difficult to trace: to which may be added, that the terms we now employ to express our feelings and passions, and all that depicts mind and its operations, are of a figurative or metaphorical origin. Instead of any word being insignificant, there is no one but may become the keystone in a sentence; and therefore a word blotted out in a perspicuous, that is, a properly constructed sentence, would render it unintelligible. To the composition of a sentence, whatever may be the thought, certain words are absolutely necessary, each containing an individual meaning; which, like a sum in addition, composed of different units, each possessing a separate and intrinsic value, may, when added together, produce the total. To those who have not attentively considered the subject, there is considerable difficulty in understanding how a determinate number of words can include the intelligence contained in a proposition or sentence: and especially how these components of separate significations can become connected for such general and comprehensive meaning. It should be recollected that such is the amazing inclosure of language, that it comprehends all the living and inanimate materials of this world, all that perception can detect, memory recall, or thought elaborate. This exposition includes the present posture of human affairs, and the movements we observe:—much that has heretofore occurred, which the characters of language have preserved unfaded from dark and remote ages: and are competent to transmit to a distant posterity, with accumulated interest: all that experience has amassed, accompanied with the consoling promises of the future, which Revelation has unfolded. The extended empire of speech, and its perpetuating characters, embrace this prodigious range; but their comprehension is exclusively limited to the human race. When words can represent all that is evident and all that is conjectural—the works of Omnipotence, and the fabrications of man— we need to seek no further for the necessary materials of thought. The difficulty that has perplexed many persons respecting the compactness and unity of intelligence that a sentence contains, principally arises from their ignorance of the precise meaning of individual words. Etymologists would employ them in their original sense, and consider themselves justified by referring to their primitive import: others would use them according to their ordinary acceptation, which may be perverted; for in the currency of language, much is defective and counterfeit: but in general the authority of writers who are accredited, however they may disagree, is adopted. The intrinsic meaning of many words, especially the particles, will appear obscure; because they are disguised abbreviations of other words, and, in some instances, are sunk so deeply, that they cannot be fathomed. A protracted life might now be consumed in the investigation of these convenient and necessary particles, including the voluminous efforts of those illustrious grammarians who have terminated their discordant labours, without arriving at their primitive signification. The chemical elements of matter have undergone various reforms, and actual revolutions, and still await ulterior confusion.

The clearness of the thought will be manifested by the perspicuity of the sentence that expresses it. Whatever may be related, is most readily comprehended, when detailed in the strict order of its occurrence. If a procession be described, the exact sequence of its train must be noted, otherwise it will become a confused mixture of persons, or a mob. The same regularity is required in the construction of a sentence; and it appears fortunate that the English language reconciles this direct location of words, on which, its conformity to natural events and human transactions principally depends. From this straight-forward expression of meaning we may expect a future excellence of composition, and a more direct elaboration of thought. This distant prospect which imagination paints, and hope promotes, can only be realized under a system where light streams uncontrolled, and the atmosphere we breathe is free. The spirit of liberty must preside where improvement is expected. When we have acquired the power and habit of original thinking, the most important part of education, the mind is emancipated, and its independence commences: we cease to be espaliers, and become standards. Hitherto we have been principally trained according to the ancient models. The Greek and Latin historians, orators, and poets, have consumed, to a great extent, the docile season of youth: when perception is active, and memory most permanently retains its various deposits, to the dereliction of the great presentations of Nature, the operations of numbers, the foundations of science, and more especially the exercise of thought. After we have quitted school, and commenced our career of profitable employment, these studies are seldom continued, and from desuetude are soon forgotten; or only revived, perhaps unaptly, in an occasional quotation. Even a living language, when not exercised, fades from the recollection. The indirect location of words which prevails in Latin, can be no model for English composition, where regular and consecutive meaning constitute the perspicuity of the sentence; and according to the reasoning that has been adopted, of the thought itself. Words, and the meaning which resides in each individual, are the only media by which our thoughts can be conveyed; and if these, which are connected by sense and subject, are so separated, or dislocated, that it becomes a puzzle to reduce them to their natural order, such distraction ought not to be considered an example for the process of thinking, and its development by composition or construction of sentences in the English language. The connexion that exists in a perspicuous sentence, is the conjunction of meaning, a further proof of the individual signification of words, and which bearing a definite sense, are selected for the purpose of that composition, which we term the process of thinking. To this connexion we are directed by the knowledge we possess of any particular subject, when we are intently occupied in its investigation, with a view to confute or confirm it, or by a more successful effort to arrive at discovery: and these acts of thought involve the continuation of meaning by the addition of words adapted to fulfil such intention.

Connexion, in a great degree, is the contrivance of our own minds, and has been frequently confounded with successive occurrences, many of which, on examination, are detected to be in no manner related; most persons link together circumstances that ought to be kept apart, and which often prove the source of unsurmountable prejudices.

It will scarcely be contended, that the order of time establishes such concatenation, although it forms the basis of historical narrative. Each portion of time must be individual and distinct, and essentially consists in its subdivisions: indeed, if we were to fuse together hours, days and years, our existence would only amount to a tedious dream. The letters of the alphabet are insulated symbols, and have no natural connexion with each other, but may be arranged to constitute words, which possess a definite meaning. Words are in the same situation, there is no connexion in a vocabulary; they resemble the individuals of our species. Each is a separate being, charged with his own propensities and peculiar character; but he may become connected with others in friendship, in interest, or as the member of a society for particular objects: he may confederate with immense bodies, for the protection of his rights, or become part of an army for the destruction of his neighbours. Thus one philosophical system, in pamphlets or in formidable volumes, endeavours to overturn another: but the words are individual, and have no tendency to associate until they are enlisted and disciplined into the composition of sentences.

When the proposition or sentence is formed, it ought to bear evidence of the most direct connexion, for the purposes of being readily comprehended and enduringly retained. From the nature of our minds, we recollect events, however unconnected, in the order of their occurrence, and we acquire by heart any passage, of level construction, with greater facility than where the natural sequence is disarranged; we repeat lines from Pope with superior fidelity than quotations from Milton.

To compress this Essay into the smallest compass, citations have been studiously avoided; yet there is a temptation to illustrate this subject by the introduction of an Epigram from Martial, *Lib. 5, Epig. 1.*

 13 14   18   15   17   16   18
"Hoc tibi Palladiæ seu collibus uteris Albæ,

 2 19 20   22   21   23   24
Cæsar et hinc Triviam prospicis inde Thetin:

 25 28   26   27   28   26
Seu tua veridicæ discunt responsa sorores,

 30   31   29 32 30 31
Plana suburbani qua cubat unda freti:

33 30 35 34 37 38 39
Seu placet Æneæ nutrix, seu filia solis,

40 42 41 41 42
Sive salutiferis candidus anxur aquis;

12 1 6 3 8 5 4
Mittimus o rerum felix tutela salusque,

7 7 12 8 10 9
Sospite quo gratum credimus esse Jovem."

The figures pointing out the "*ordo verborum*" are according to the subjoined interpretation of Mons. Collesson, who prepared this Delphine edition. The same figures have been placed where the adjective agrees with the substantive or pronoun; and for this clew to the consecutive arrangement of these disbanded and dispersed members of the sentence, some young gentlemen at school, and many who have finished their education, will be under considerable obligations.

It is of considerable moment that this question should be fully discussed in order to be finally determined. The groundwork is physiological, the superstructure involves some moral considerations: and the conclusions will have an extensive influence on the system of education that ought to be adopted. If the perceptions of the eye, and its associated phantasms, or memorial visions, under the name of Ideas, are to be viewed as the effective materials of our Thoughts; such inference is directly confuted by the instances of those born blind, and continue through life without sight, and who must necessarily be deficient of such materials. If Thought be the result of any immediate spiritual dictation, which the difficulty of accounting for it without such mysterious agency, has led many to suppose: and of which we are not conscious, the responsibility of our species is destroyed. If Thought be effected by the selection and arrangement of words, each of which possesses a definite meaning, and is capable when conjoined with other words, of adding to their significance: of which process, and the individual steps that compose it, we *are* conscious under due attention, the mystery vanishes, and the act of thinking becomes unfolded in the progressive formation of a perspicuous sentence.

FOOTNOTES:

[1] The eye is the only organ of sense that affords a connected phantasm, vision or Idea. In the other senses, there is a memorial connection, by which the perception is recognised as having previously occurred, and consequently a consciousness of former perception. Without these adjuncts the repetition of these perceptions would be useless as instruments of knowledge. Avoiding a lengthened detail concerning the other senses, it will be sufficient to instance the olfactory organ. If we scent the essences of rose or jasmine, on the second presentation, they are recognised as having occurred before: should we have smelled the same perfumes from the living plants that exhale them, and by the *eye* noticed them, we should experience a phantasm or Idea of the figure of the plants, but there would be no phantasm of the odour. The excitation of the phantasm associated with the perception, and the recollection of the perception without the phantasm, by the attribution of a name, is, for the present, purposely concealed.

[2] Modification. A word of useless application, unless the *modus in quo agit*, be defined.

[3] Of the supposed operations of these Ideas, and the purposes to which they are subjected, a few, among abundant instances, are selected from Mr. Locke's Essay. "Some Ideas *forwardly* offer themselves to all men's understanding; some sorts of truths result from any Ideas, as soon as the mind puts *them* into propositions: other Truths require a *train* of Ideas *placed in order*."—*Vol.* I. *p.* 63.

"When the understanding is once stored with these simple Ideas, it has the power to *repeat*, *compare*, and *unite* them, even to an almost infinite variety, and so can make at pleasure *new* complex Ideas."—*Vol.* I. *p.* 81.

"The next operation we may observe in the mind about its Ideas, is Composition, whereby it puts together several of those simple ones it has received from sensation and reflection, and *combines* them into complex ones."—*Vol.* I. *p.* 118.

"If either by any sudden very strong impression, or long fixing his fancy upon one sort of thoughts, *incoherent* Ideas have been *cemented* together so powerfully, as to remain united."—*Vol.* I. *p.* 121.

"But there are degree of Madness as of folly, the disorderly *jumbling* Ideas together, in some more, and some less." *Vol.* I. *p.* 122.

"The acts of the mind wherein it exerts its power over its simple Ideas, are chiefly three. 1st. Combining several simple Ideas into one *compound one*, and *thus* all complex Ideas are made. The second, is bringing *two Ideas*, whether simple or complex together, and *setting* them by one another, so as to take a view of them *at once*, without uniting them into one; by which way it gets all its Ideas of relations. The third, is *separating* them from all other Ideas that *accompany* them in their real existence; this is called Abstraction."— *Vol.* I. *p.* 124.

[4] The acquirement of language does not wholly consist in the imitation of the word, but likewise in the comprehension that the articulate sound is the representative of the object perceived. There are some persons of defective intellect that I have seen, whose hearing was perfect, and who could whistle some tunes, but who were unable to learn their native language so as to understand what

was said to them, and consequently incompetent to afford an answer. In this particular they approximate to the state of animals.

[5] "Nec missas audire queunt, nec reddere voces."

[6] On consulting the Concordance of Cruden, it does not appear that the word Idea, is to be found in our Translations of the Old and New Testament. Cruden, although deemed a Lunatic, was a man of persevering research and scrupulous accuracy.

[7] It is very probable that Martial, in his eulogy of the Roman Notarius, may have exceeded the actual performance.

> "Currant verba licet, manus est velocior illis:
> Nondum linga suum, dextra peregit opus."
> *Lib. 14, Epig. 208.*

[8] In imitation of the Auburn (American) prison, the Middlesex magistrates, in their judicial wisdom, have adopted an entirely opposite system; by imposing an awful silence in their house of correction. This penance must press sorely on the criminals of

the softer sex, to whom tea and conversation (errors excepted) constitute the principal comforts of life. Catullus seems to allude to this infernal art of exasperating the miseries of incarceration.

"Nulla fugæ ratio, nulla spes: OMNIA MUTA,
Omnia sunt deserta: ostentant omnia Lethum."

www.ingramcontent.com/pod-product-compliance
Lightning Source LLC
Chambersburg PA
CBHW050758240726
48654CB00008B/547